THE SWIM

Hits The Road

Gill Smith

Published by Purple Parrot Publishing (in association with Ainslie & Fishwick Publishing Ltd).

Printed in the United Kingdom.
First Printing, 2019.

ISBN: Print (Soft cover): 978-1-912677-22-1
          Ebook: 978-1-912677-23-8

Book design by Viv Ainslie

www.purpleparrotpublishing.co.uk

The Swim Taxi started life on Twitter to raise awareness of the Swim Family Smith's fundraising #swimforhearts campaign in aid of the British Heart Foundation.

Following an out-of-the-blue poolside heart attack when aged just 43, Swim Mum decided to quit her career as a Deputy Headteacher and focus on getting well, growing the family performance mindset swim business and supporting the Swim Daughters to chase their swimming dreams.

Stunned that her Twitter musings don't seem to put too many people off, this lighthearted book of anecdotes shines an honest light on the trials and tribulations of life as a swim parent.

A percentage of all sales will support the family BHF fundraising campaign.

WE THANK YOU!

gill x

www.theswimtaxi.com
www.connectswim.co.uk

www.justgiving.com/fundraising/swimforhearts

Have you packed your bag?
Have you got your water bottle?
Hurry up, we're leaving in 5 minutes.
No, we aren't stopping at McDonalds.
Repeat. Repeat. Repeat. FFS.

#swimtaxi #autopilot

Dos & Don'ts with a teen swimmer:
Don't:
- Ask how training went
- Get excited when on blocks
- Cheer when racing
- Wave at them when with mates
- Remind them to drink water
- Sing out loud in the Swim Taxi
Do:
- Go ahead and do all the above anyway
#embarrassingparents

Swim Mum appreciates the enormity of what these Swim Kids do day in, day out.

Swim Mum does not appreciate the enormity of the food bill each week or the sibling competitiveness over a packet of sodding Jaffa cakes.

#swimmum #swimbills

Yesterday, the rankings site must have been on fire. Swim Mum is surprised it didn't crash.

Cornered by obsessed swim parents declaring their child's regional position.

#eyeroll #swimmum

Don't judge but Swim Mum has just seen the programme for county champs. The first things scanned through for were:

1) Do we have any mornings off?

2) Where the nearest off site get outta there cafe is.

3) What time it all finishes.

Be honest, you'd do the same.

#swimmumlife

Swim Mum needs to do an urgent food shop.

Swim Mum is too tired to go out and wonders if the Halloween buckets full of Haribos, M&M's and Skittles will do her Swim Daughters any real nutritional harm?

#burnitoff #swimparentproblems #swimmumlife

Swim Mum better get her shit together.
She's buggering off for the weekend &
Swim Dad is in charge:

• Training • arena league • time trials
• kits • puppy • meals • grandparents
• hormonal outbursts to coordinate

Swim Mum packs her glad rags and
prosecco and smiles sweetly to herself.

#laters

County champs.

Swim Mum's loving the heady mix of teenage hormones, stifling chlorinated air and warm pasta eaten from stained Tupperware.

Does life get much better than this?

#counties #livingthedream

Apparently success in the water doesn't come from shortcuts.

Swim Mum loves a bloody shortcut.

Fast forwarding the 'I'm a celeb' adverts, choosing the alternative faster route on the sat nav & microwaving the dinners.

No wonder she packed in swimming.

#swimshortcuts

If you're not up now scrolling and posting on Twitter at 5.30am on a Saturday, are you even a Swim Parent?

#swimsleep #swimalarm

The Swim Parents eagerly giving feedback to little Timmy after his race get Swim Mum's best eye roll and a prayer that he gets a McDonald's on the way home instead of a protein shake and his pic on Face Boast.

#poortimmy #swimparents

Swim Daughter 1 is looking forward to the weekend club mini meet.

If she masters getting her racesuit over her butt in less than 10 minutes, she's a total winner in Swim Mum's eyes.

#swimchallenge #swimmersproblems

If you haven't been driving around for
at least a couple of weeks with screwed
up county champs programmes,
dirty water bottles,
McDonald's wrappers and a kit
bag in your taxi,
are you even a Swim Parent?

#theswimtaxi

Swim Mum's considering applying for a second mortgage to prop up the eye-watering amount of money spent so far this swim season.

Need she say more?

#rolloncounciltaxfreemonths
#swimfamilysmith #swimlife

Swim Mum's looking forward to spending
time with the old folks today & showing
them how to access the shared cloud
swimming photos, explaining LC & SC
conversions and directing them
to dates & live streaming links
for counties.

Again.

#swimgran

Swim Mum is working away and wonders for a minute if she'll miss doing the swim run tonight.

She checks in to her lovely hotel, settles in the king size and picks up the room service menu.

Sorry, what swim run!?

#laters #overtoyouswimdad

This morning the Swim Daughters created a twerking routine.

Allegedly this is, in their words, important to help improve their fly.

Swim Mum cannot find ANY part of this that is right.

#swimmum #swimparent
#swimproblems #kidsoftoday

Swim Mum can't help but swear lightly under her breath when she hears yet another excuse that little *insert name* isn't well today ...so 'we're not expecting anything at this meet.'

FFS.
Stay at home then and give your swimmer a bloody rest.

#itsnotheolympics #swimparents

Swim Mum can't recall the last time she crossed the pool threshold in daylight.

She's considering installing a 10,000 lux light lamp in the swim taxi as she subscribes and saves Vitamin D tablets on Amazon prime.

#swimmum #swimtaxi
#swimparent #lightdeprived

Swim Mum is back home
from working away.

Unsurprisingly the cupboards are bare
and the rush is on to get to training.

It's okay, she never fails to marvel at the
speed at which Swim Daughters can
demolish a Greggs pasty or three.

#swimnutrition #swimfamilysmith

Don't feel bad...
We stopped at KFC too after the meet.
Mostly because Swim Mum craved it.
But also because it's not the Olympics.

#swimmumwins

First kid at swim meet: Bag check: new racesuit, fab goggles, healthy snacks, don't eat sweets, drink water, pop up & see us, wave lots, pls don't worry.

2nd kid: Hey coach, here's my kid. Complete with hand me down everything. Have a ball.

doesn't see them again for 6 hours

Swim Parenting is:

Committing big time to the programme
and then praying for: chlorine issues, pool
poo or broken heating to get
a surprise session off.
Especially tonight.

Repeat, repeat, repeat.

#canwehaveanightoff #swimfamilysmith

Counties weekend 1 done...

Swim Daughter 1 has swiftly returned to watching the Friends Box Set, declaring how she deserves a county trophy for sacrificing Netflix for the entire weekend.

#swimlife #countychamps

Spearheading is the greatest spanner
in the works when it comes to
explaining what's going on.

#swimlife #swimcoach

Swim Mum marvels at how quickly the Swim Daughters can multiply in 25s and 50s.

Chuck in the 33s though and it's pure bedlam.

#swimmaths #swimforhearts

Feeling like running away from
the 400IM today at counties;

Swim Daughter 1 has to be gently
reminded that she actually can't run.

#swimmersdontrun #mermaids

Swim Mum wonders which website you can order those perfect swim kids from.

You know the smiling organised ones packing their own stuff, stretching off at every opportunity, lovingly taking care of each other & willingly munching on curly kale & Brazil nuts?

#notinthishouse

Water bottles.

Missing lids.

You are the swim family equivalent
of odd socks.

FFS.

#swimpuzzles #swimlife

Today the Swim Daughters were astonished to discover that wearing a bobble hat after training helps keep their head warm during the walk back to the car.

Fancy that, thinks Swim Mum.

#swimmum #swimwarmth

Swim Dad asked why Swim Mum had bought three massive boxes of Weetabix.

What sort of stupid question is that?

#swimhunger

Sorting the Tupperware cupboard
ready for meet weekends so Swim Mum
can experience unusual feelings
of being organised.

Feels remarkably like a
game of bloody Tetris.

#tupperwarehell

If you don't point out several times a day to everyone how tired you are because you did the morning swim run, are you even a Swim Parent?

#swimcomplaints #swimparentlife

Swim Daughter 1 presented Swim Mum with her hoodie that has lost the pull strings up inside the hood.

So, tonight she's looking at a 2 hour project, minimum.

FFS.

#swimhoodie #swimproject

Swim Dad has woken up bright and early for Swim Daughter's extra training session.

This has pissed Swim Mum off as she quite fancied a lie in, but is now wide-awake on bloody Twitter.

#lifeofaswimmum #swimparent #rudeawakening

You know what's better than gin?

County champs over for another year,
the Swim Daughters are fast asleep,
washing done, clean bedding, coach
has given a rest day tomorrow and
a massive gin.

#feetupginpoured

#fridayswimfreedom

Let's just tell you this again
non-swim parents.

Swim caps are not to keep hair dry.

#swimmersproblems

Swim Mum heaves a sigh of relief.

It's Friday.

Even better, it's a swim meet
free weekend.

Goodness, they might get outside and
avert the onset of rickets after all.

#vitaminD #swimlife

Are you even a Swim Parent if you don't own a drawer full of broken goggles, a mahoosive collection of random swim hats and a Tupperware cupboard like hell on Earth?

#swimparentlife #tupperwarehell

I haven't heard any unsolicited
swimming advice from non-qualified
parents in a while.

Said no Swim Parent ever.

#swimlife #swimparent #swimcoach
#swimmum #swimdad
#swimmerproblems

Swim Mum worries about the anything beige or dairy diet of the Swim Daughters.

She thanks God for pizza: tomato sauce bringing a dash of colour and a hint of nutritional value.

With lashings of pepperoni.

Phew...

#swimnutrition

So Swim Dad is starting to measure the enjoyment factor of a gala by the cost of the races.

It's like he's on bloody holiday getting excited over the price of a beer.

- Only 2 euros a pint; brilliant holiday
- Only £3.50 a race; fecking awesome gala

#swimmortgage

Swim Daughter 2 is learning the
hard way already.

Today she learnt that trying to explain
swimming at counties to her
class during show and tell
is basically the same
as talking to the wall.

#didyouwin #swimmersproblems

Swim Mum is asking if there is anyone out there with a burning desire to do her swim run tonight?

Much as she loves them, she enjoys lying on the sofa, watching Strictly on catch up and drinking a couple of gins far more.

#swimgin #myturn

It's time for Swim Mum to get her arse into gear and get organised ahead of 3 weekends of counties.

Big shop time.

Pasta. Pasta. Pasta.

Wine.

There. That'll do.

#swimfamilysmith

Afraid to try her jeans on after over
consumption of pigs in blankets,
Swim Mum's grateful that at least
she doesn't have to attempt
squashing her butt into a racesuit.

#swimmumproblems

If you aren't paying a high level of attention to detail trying to sneak all things nutritional into your child's swim diet, are you even a Swim Parent?

Unless it's straight after a meet when you just think f*** it and pull straight into Mcdonald's drive thru without hesitation.

#swimwins

When Swim Mum texts teen
Swim Daughter the very exciting news
that she's picked for Arena A Final
in Cardiff, uses happy dance gifs
and lots of congrats, and all
she gets as a reply is…

'K'

#swimteen #detailedresponse

Are you even a Swim Parent if your
swim teen isn't mad at you
74% of the time,
mostly regarding lack of
food in the cupboards?

#swimhunger #swimhangry

'Mum, seriously, pasta... Again?'

'Yep.'

Swim Mum loves it when a well thought out culinary plan comes together.

#swimnosh #feedemup

More books, resources and merchandise from
The Swim Taxi coming soon.

Follow The Swim Taxi' on Twitter, Facebook and Instagram.

@theswimtaxi

@theswimtaxi

@theswimtaxi

And if you haven't seen The Swim Taxi blog, check out:
www.connectswim.co.uk/blog-2

CONNECT SWIM

www.theswimtaxi.com
www.connectswim.co.uk

CPSIA information can be obtained
at www.ICGtesting.com
Printed in the USA
BVHW020920170919
558548BV00016B/194/P

9 781912 677221